Sarcasms, Visions Fugitives
and Other Short Works for Piano

Sergei Prokofiev

Notes by
Dmitry Feofanov

DOVER PUBLICATIONS, INC.
Mineola, New York

Bibliographical Note

This Dover edition, first published in 2000, is a new compilation of works originally published separately in authoritative early editions. Opp. 2, 3, 4, 11, 12, and 17 were originally published by P. Jurgenson, Leipzig, n.d. [1911–1915]. Opp. 22, 31, 32 and 33 were originally published by A. Gutheil, Moscow (Breitkopf & Härtel, Leipzig), 1922.
Dmitry Feofanov's notes have been adapted from prefatory texts originally written for two Prokofiev piano editions that are no longer available.
We are indebted to Dr. Olga Ushitskaya, former archivist for the Moscow Conservatory Library, for her assistance in finding and compiling these works.

International Standard Book Number: 0-486-41091-9

Manufactured in the United States of America
Dover Publications, Inc., 31 East 2nd Street, Mineola, N.Y. 11501

CONTENTS

INTRODUCTION

Prokofiev never had much luck with critics, but the listening public long ago embraced many of his greatest works. And it could be claimed that in the field of piano music Prokofiev's works actually offer *the best* that the twentieth century has to offer. No modern composer, with the notable exceptions of Debussy and Ravel, has ever approached his combined quality and quantity. Bartók may be his equal in the field of the concerto, but his sonata does not compare to the towering masterpieces of Prokofiev's Sixth, Seventh and Eighth. Barber has a sonata to match, but not a concerto. With the exception of his *Petrushka* transcriptions, Stravinsky's piano works are not even in the running.

This collection, which comprises 56 piano pieces in a single volume, provides a unique opportunity to trace the composer's development over his formative first decade of piano composition, 1909–1919. Most of these works are little gems of unmistakable originality.

FOUR ÉTUDES, OP. 2. Prokofiev himself considered these études a breakthrough in his compositional language. Following the brooding and fairly conventional First Piano Sonata, they represent a deliberate attempt at innovation. The most interesting are the third and the fourth. The third is notable for its inventive piano writing and triple counterpoint, clearly displaying the influence of Prokofiev's one-time teacher Sergey Taneyev. The fourth is written in a toccata style, anticipating such early-period warhorses as *Diabolical suggestion* and the *Toccata*.

FOUR PIECES, OP. 3. Some of these are reworkings of pieces begun as early as 1907. Only after jazzing them up with spicy harmonies was Prokofiev sufficiently content with the results to perform and publish them. (Some of the pieces of Op. 12 reveal such belated "Prokofievization" as well. For example, the marches of both opuses initially were written in a fairly conventional idiom, quite unlike their final form.) Like Op. 2, however, the language is not yet natural, although texturally the pieces "look" right. From the lyricism of *Tale* to the scherzando style of *Joke* to the directness of *March* to the frantic frenzy of *Phantom*, all the common moods of Prokofiev's mature style are already present.

FOUR PIECES, OP. 4 (excerpts). This is the first of the piano works where Prokofiev's gift is in full bloom, showing the unmistakable originality and harmonic inventiveness so characteristic of Prokofiev in his prime. *Reminiscences* displays Prokofiev's growing mastery in handling dramatic climaxes and his fondness for ecstatic ostinato outbursts, which feature so prominently in his later works (e.g., *The Fiery Angel*). *Diabolical suggestion* (the English title that does not quite do justice to the Russian word *Navaždenie*) is also top-notch,

and a staple of the virtuoso repertoire. In this work, I do not recommend following the original distribution of the hands, which calls for too much "left over right" playing. Rather, playing without crossing the hands seems to work better.

TOCCATA, OP. 11. This famous piece is masterfully constructed from two simple motives (the first a repeated note, the second a minor triad). A performance note: Though it has become traditional to play the piece as fast as possible, this is a mistake. The fast tempo fails to allow for the "marcato" in the "Allegro marcato" indication—it is not possible to play heavy "marcato" very fast. Furthermore, a light, brisk tempo will preclude the performer's making the sharp accelerando that Prokofiev explicitly demands on the last page.

TEN PIECES, OP. 12. An extremely attractive collection, containing some of Prokofiev's most popular short pieces, such as the famous *Prelude*.

March. A delightful and witty piece, anticipating in its middle part the march theme of the hunters from *Peter and the Wolf* almost note for note.

Gavotte. The first of the stylized dances Prokofiev so delighted in writing. Unfortunately, this piece is overburdened with contrapuntal work, unlike its more successful cousins, the gavottes from the *Classical Symphony* and Op. 32. The performer is faced with the formidable task of lightening up the texture, while dealing with octaves, widely spaced chords, voicing problems and awkward hand distribution.

Rigaudon. An amusing case of the use of the *Petrushka* chord, but otherwise a tad below par. In fairness, an assertive and constructivist piece, which works well as an encore.

Mazurka. This formalist experiment, written entirely in fourths, is less successful. Occasionally such tricks work (*e.g.,* Debussy's prelude in thirds), but here Prokofiev does not yet have Debussy's melodic inventiveness and mastery of form.

Capriccio. This piece is written in the "new" folk style that Prokofiev cultivated in some of his most successful compositions (*e.g.,* the Third Piano Concerto.) *Capriccio* is reminiscent of the scene in the monastery from *Boris Godunov* in which Pimen inscribes events in the chronicle. The tone-painting in the piece imitates the sound of a pen on parchment. With this picture in mind, the piece enchants performers and listeners alike.

Legend. Yet another of the folk-idiom pieces, and quite successful.

Prelude (Harp). This needs no introduction. It is perhaps the most popular among the Op. 12 pieces, and its popularity is well deserved. It is a charming example of Prokofiev's diatonic style, in addition to being a clever imitation of a harp style.

Allemande. This actually sounds like a second gavotte, and again, like the *March,* brings to mind *Peter and the Wolf* in its middle part. An engaging piece that deserves to be heard more often.

Humorous scherzo (for four bassoons). To produce the effect of bassoons, the performer should use pedal very sparingly. Redistributing the hands in the middle part will help achieve a good legato. An easygoing manner and a sense of humor are a must.

Scherzo. Perhaps the most technically difficult of all the shorter pieces. One should not attempt to play this piece unless one is prepared to strive for a true *vivacissimo,* which requires countless practice hours. The result, however, should be well worth the trouble. The *Scherzo* is a remarkably effective piece, which finally puts all the experimental devices of the earlier works together into a cogent whole. Here we find harmonic touches that are especially characteristic of Prokofiev, such as quick and assured modulations into distant keys, convincing though unmercifully difficult counterpoint, and explosive rhythmic vitality. The pianist should bring out the hemiolas, which undermine the basically square rhythmic structure of the piece.

SARCASMS, OP. 17.
In this cycle Prokofiev reveals the caustic and mocking part of his personality. While some of the pieces are not quite polished (nos. 3 and 4) and some are not entirely engaging (no. 2), the cycle as a whole has a raw, overwhelming power.

The interpretation of *Sarcasms* requires grand dramatic gestures, and it should be played in a fanciful, capricious, rubato manner. An unfortunate myth has grown up around Prokofiev's music, requiring modern performers to play it with machinelike precision. The proponents of this approach fail to consider that, as a performer, Prokofiev was a product of the same school as Arthur Schnabel, being a direct pianistic descendant of Theodor Leschetizky (through both of Prokofiev's piano teachers, Alexander Winkler and especially Leschetizky's wife, Anna Esipova). Rubato playing was in his blood. One need only compare the composer's own eye-opening recording of the Third Piano Concerto with modern sewing-machine imitations to appreciate the difference. Recommended, both as individual pieces and as a cycle.

VISIONS FUGITIVES, OP. 22.
This cycle of preludes contains some of Prokofiev's most attractive and unassuming piano writing. The title, which is literally translated "Evanescences," is meant to convey the idea of a single fleeting mood or character in each piece. The cycle has an unusual ending; the wayward unreality of the last piece suggests a stunned reaction to the preceding one, which is said to be a descriptive response to witnessing gunfire in the streets during the Russian Revolution.

Though these pieces are customarily played in groups of three to six, the cycle should be performed in its entirety more often. It takes only a little over twenty minutes to perform. As with the Third Concerto, the performer will profit from consulting Prokofiev's own recording, illuminating in its humor and abundant use of rubato. The performer should be warned, however, against taking any of the strained or exaggerated liberties that are occasionally conspicuous in modern recordings. In performance and composition, Prokofiev tried to achieve simplicity above all.

TALES OF THE OLD GRANDMOTHER, OP. 31.
The *Tales* are wonderful little pieces, sometimes not quite developed texturally, but charming and sweet nevertheless. Particularly notable is the second, anticipating the melodic wonders of *Cinderella* and *Romeo and Juliet.*

FOUR PIECES, OP. 32.
An underrated collection, known mostly for its excellent *Gavotte.* The *Minuet* is also absolutely first-rate. *Dance* presents more of a problem of first reading; yet one can grow to accept the piece, bizarre as it may be, on its own terms. The *Waltz* is a masterly lyric miniature, even though its language seems to rely on rather generic chromatic harmony and lacks Prokofiev's unmistakable touches. Still, its hypnotic, dreamlike imagery makes an immediate impact on listeners. The performer should not fail to note the similarity to its better-known relative, the dreamlike waltz from the Sixth Piano Sonata.

MARCH AND SCHERZO, OP. 33ter
(from *The love for three oranges*). Prokofiev's formidable piano technique served him especially well in the piano music he transcribed from his scores for opera, ballet, orchestra and chamber ensembles. These remarkable transcriptions vary according to their purpose. Some are faithful reductions of the originals, intended to make the music accessible to a wider audience. Others, however—like this *March and Scherzo*—are intricate elaborations of their original sources, enriched texturally and musically.

The *March* became for Prokofiev what the *Prelude in C-sharp minor* had been for Rachmaninoff. Unlike his world-famous compatriot, however, Prokofiev never grew tired of the piece and, by all accounts, performed the *March* with gusto.

The *Scherzo,* another orchestral episode from the opera, is typical of the composer's scherzando style.

Dmitry Feofanov

DMITRY FEOFANOV was the top prize-winner in the 1982 University of Maryland International Piano Competition. He is the editor of *Rare Masterpieces of Russian Piano Music* (Dover, 1984). In 1989–90, in commemoration of the Prokofiev centennial, he performed Prokofiev's complete piano works in a series of five recitals in Chicago.

Sarcasms, Visions Fugitives
and Other Short Works for Piano

Étude

No. 1 of *Four études*, Op. 2

Étude

No. 2 of *Four études*, Op. 2

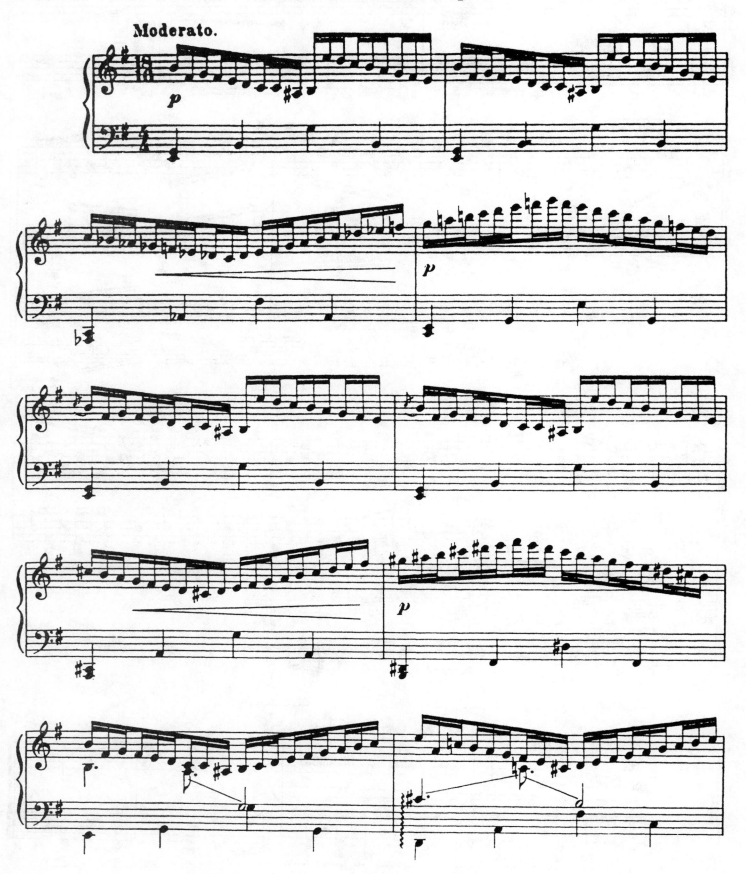

Étude

No. 3 of *Four études*, Op. 2

Étude

No. 4 of *Four études*, Op. 2

Tale

No. 1 of *Four pieces*, Op. 3

Joke

No. 2 of *Four pieces*, Op. 3

March

No. 3 of *Four pieces*, Op. 3

Phantom

No. 4 of *Four pieces*, Op. 3

from **FOUR PIECES, Op. 4**
(1908–12)

Reminiscences
No. 1 of *Four pieces*, Op. 4

Diabolical suggestion

No. 4 of *Four pieces,* Op. 4

Prestissimo fantastico.

42 / "Diabolical suggestion," Op. 4, No. 4

Toccata

Op. 11 (1912)

(1906–13)

March

No. 1 of *Ten pieces*, Op. 12

Gavotte

No. 2 of *Ten pieces*, Op. 12

Rigaudon

No. 3 of *Ten pieces*, Op. 12

Mazurka

No. 4 of *Ten pieces*, Op. 12

Capriccio

No. 5 of *Ten pieces*, Op. 12

Legend

No. 6 of *Ten pieces*, Op. 12

Prelude

(Harp)

No. 7 of *Ten pieces*, Op. 12

Vivo e delicato.

Allemande

No. 8 of *Ten pieces*, Op. 12

Allegro risoluto.

Humorous scherzo
(for four bassoons)
No. 9 of *Ten pieces*, Op. 12

Allegro.

Scherzo

No. 10 of *Ten pieces*, Op. 12

SARCASMS, Op. 17
(1912–14)

1.

2.

3.

of 5 *Sarcasms*, Op. 17

Allegro precipitato.

4.

of 5 *Sarcasms,* Op. 17

5.

of 5 *Sarcasms*, Op. 17

Precipitosissimo.

VISIONS FUGITIVES, Op. 22

(1915–17)

1.

2.

of 20 *Visions fugitives*, Op. 22

3.

4.

of 20 *Visions fugitives*, Op. 22

5.

of 20 *Visions fugitives,* Op. 22

6.

of 20 *Visions fugitives,* Op. 22

7. (Harp)
of 20 *Visions fugitives*, Op. 22

8.

of 20 *Visions fugitives,* Op. 22

9.

Allegretto tranquillo.

10.

[Ridiculosamente]

11.

of 20 *Visions fugitives*, Op. 22

13.

of 20 *Visions fugitives, Op. 22*

14.

of 20 *Visions fugitives,* Op. 22

15.

of 20 *Visions fugitives*, Op. 22

16.

of 20 *Visions fugitives*, Op. 22

17.

of 20 *Visions fugitives,* Op. 22

Poetico.

18.

19.

of 20 *Visions fugitives*, Op. 22

Presto agitatissimo e molto accentuato.

20.

of 20 *Visions fugitives*, Op. 22

TALES OF THE OLD GRANDMOTHER, Op. 31

(1918)

1.

2.

of 4 *Tales of the old grandmother*, Op. 31

3.

of 4 *Tales of the old grandmother*, Op. 31

4.

of 4 *Tales of the old grandmother,* Op. 31

Pochissimo più animato.

senza agitazione   *un poco cresc.*

cresc.

March

From the opera *The love for three oranges*, Op. 33 (1919)
Piano transcription by the composer, Op. 33*ter* (1922)

Scherzo

From the opera *The love for three oranges,* Op. 33 (1919)
Piano transcription by the composer, Op. 33*ter* (1922)

Dance

No. 1 of *Four pieces,* Op. 32

Allegretto. *Con eleganza.*

Minuet

No. 2 of *Four pieces*, Op. 32

Allegro moderato.

Gavotte

No. 3 of *Four pieces*, Op. 32

Waltz

No. 4 of *Four pieces,* Op. 32

END OF EDITION

Dover Piano and Keyboard Editions

THE WELL-TEMPERED CLAVIER: Books I and II, Complete, Johann Sebastian Bach. All 48 preludes and fugues in all major and minor keys. Authoritative Bach-Gesellschaft edition. Explanation of ornaments in English, tempo indications, music corrections. 208pp. 9⅜ × 12¼. 24532-2 Pa. **$9.95**

KEYBOARD MUSIC, J. S. Bach. Bach-Gesellschaft edition. For harpsichord, piano, other keyboard instruments. English Suites, French Suites, Six Partitas, Goldberg Variations, Two-Part Inventions, Three-Part Sinfonias. 312pp. 8⅛ × 11. 22360-4 Pa. **$12.95**

ITALIAN CONCERTO, CHROMATIC FANTASIA AND FUGUE AND OTHER WORKS FOR KEYBOARD, Johann Sebastian Bach. Sixteen of Bach's best-known, most-performed and most-recorded works for the keyboard, reproduced from the authoritative Bach-Gesellschaft edition. 112pp. 9 × 12. 25387-2 Pa. **$8.95**

COMPLETE KEYBOARD TRANSCRIPTIONS OF CONCERTOS BY BAROQUE COMPOSERS, Johann Sebastian Bach. Sixteen concertos by Vivaldi, Telemann and others, transcribed for solo keyboard instruments. Bach-Gesellschaft edition. 128pp. 9⅜ × 12¼. 25529-8 Pa. **$9.95**

ORGAN MUSIC, J. S. Bach. Bach-Gesellschaft edition. 93 works. 6 Trio Sonatas, German Organ Mass, Orgelbüchlein, Six Schubler Chorales, 18 Choral Preludes. 357pp. 8⅛ × 11. 22359-0 Pa. **$13.95**

COMPLETE PRELUDES AND FUGUES FOR ORGAN, Johann Sebastian Bach. All 25 of Bach's complete sets of preludes and fugues (i.e. compositions written as pairs), from the authoritative Bach-Gesellschaft edition. 168pp. 8⅜ × 11. 24816-X Pa. **$11.95**

TOCCATAS, FANTASIAS, PASSACAGLIA AND OTHER WORKS FOR ORGAN, J. S. Bach. Over 20 best-loved works including Toccata and Fugue in D Minor, BWV 565; Passacaglia and Fugue in C Minor, BWV 582, many more. Bach-Gesellschaft edition. 176pp. 9 × 12. 25403-8 Pa. **$10.95**

TWO- AND THREE-PART INVENTIONS, J. S. Bach. Reproduction of original autograph ms. Edited by Eric Simon. 62pp. 8⅛ × 11. 21982-8 Pa. **$8.95**

THE 36 FANTASIAS FOR KEYBOARD, Georg Philipp Telemann. Graceful compositions by 18th-century master. 1923 Breslauer edition. 80pp. 8⅛ × 11. 25365-1 Pa. **$6.95**

GREAT KEYBOARD SONATAS, Carl Philipp Emanuel Bach. Comprehensive two-volume edition contains 51 sonatas by second, most important son of Johann Sebastian Bach. Originality, rich harmony, delicate workmanship. Authoritative French edition. Total of 384pp. 8⅜ × 11¼.
Series I 24853-4 Pa. **$11.95**
Series II 24854-2 Pa. **$10.95**

KEYBOARD WORKS/Series One: Ordres I–XIII; Series Two: Ordres XIV–XXVII and Miscellaneous Pieces, François Couperin. Over 200 pieces. Reproduced directly from edition prepared by Johannes Brahms and Friedrich Chrysander. Total of 496pp. 8⅛ × 11.
Series I 25795-9 Pa. **$12.95**
Series II 25796-7 Pa. **$11.95**

KEYBOARD WORKS FOR SOLO INSTRUMENTS, G. F. Handel. 35 neglected works from Handel's vast oeuvre, originally jotted down as improvisations. Includes Eight Great Suites, others. New sequence. 174pp. 9⅜ × 12¼. 24338-9 Pa. **$10.95**

WORKS FOR ORGAN AND KEYBOARD, Jan Pieterszoon Sweelinck. Nearly all of early Dutch composer's difficult-to-find keyboard works. Chorale variations; toccatas, fantasias; variations on secular, dance tunes. Also, incomplete and/or modified works, plus fantasia by John Bull. 272pp. 9 × 12. 24935-2 Pa. **$14.95**

ORGAN WORKS, Dietrich Buxtehude. Complete organ works of extremely influential pre-Bach composer. Toccatas, preludes, chorales, more. Definitive Breitkopf & Härtel edition. 320pp. 8⅜ × 11¼. (Available in U.S. only) 25682-0 Pa. **$16.95**

THE FUGUES ON THE MAGNIFICAT FOR ORGAN OR KEYBOARD, Johann Pachelbel. 94 pieces representative of Pachelbel's magnificent contribution to keyboard composition; can be played on the organ, harpsichord or piano. 100pp. 9 × 12. (Available in U.S. only) 25037-7 Pa. **$8.95**

MY LADY NEVELLS BOOKE OF VIRGINAL MUSIC, William Byrd. 42 compositions in modern notation from 1591 ms. For any keyboard instrument. 245pp. 8⅛ × 11. 22246-2 Pa. **$16.95**

ELIZABETH ROGERS HIR VIRGINALL BOOKE, edited with calligraphy by Charles J. F. Cofone. All 112 pieces from noted 1656 manuscript, most never before published. Composers include Thomas Brewer, William Byrd, Orlando Gibbons, etc. 125pp. 9 × 12. 23138-0 Pa. **$13.95**

THE FITZWILLIAM VIRGINAL BOOK, edited by J. Fuller Maitland, W. B. Squire. Famous early 17th-century collection of keyboard music, 300 works by Morley, Byrd, Bull, Gibbons, etc. Modern notation. Total of 938pp. 8⅜ × 11. Two-vol. set. 21068-5, 21069-3 Pa. **$37.90**

GREAT KEYBOARD SONATAS, Series I and Series II, Domenico Scarlatti. 78 of the most popular sonatas reproduced from the G. Ricordi edition edited by Alessandro Longo. Total of 320pp. 8⅜ × 11¼.
Series I 24996-4 Pa. **$9.95**
Series II 25003-2 Pa. **$9.95**

COMPLETE PIANO SONATAS, Joseph Haydn. 52 sonatas reprinted from authoritative Breitkopf & Härtel edition. Extremely clear and readable; ample space for notes, analysis. 464pp. 9⅜ × 12¼. 24726-0 Pa. **$13.95**
24727-9 Pa. **$13.95**

BAGATELLES, RONDOS AND OTHER SHORTER WORKS FOR PIANO, Ludwig van Beethoven. Most popular and most performed shorter works, including Rondo a capriccio in G and Andante in F. Breitkopf & Härtel edition. 128pp. 9⅜ × 12¼. 25392-9 Pa. **$8.95**

COMPLETE VARIATIONS FOR SOLO PIANO, Ludwig van Beethoven. Contains all 21 sets of Beethoven's piano variations, including the extremely popular *Diabelli Variations, Op. 120.* 240pp. 9⅜ × 12¼. 25188-8 Pa. **$12.95**

COMPLETE PIANO SONATAS, Ludwig van Beethoven. All sonatas in fine Schenker edition, with fingering, analytical material. One of best modern editions. 615pp. 9 × 12. Two-vol. set. 23134-8, 23135-6 Pa. **$25.90**

COMPLETE SONATAS FOR PIANOFORTE SOLO, Franz Schubert. All 15 sonatas. Breitkopf and Härtel edition. 293pp. 9⅜ × 12¼. 22647-6 Pa. **$14.95**

DANCES FOR SOLO PIANO, Franz Schubert. Over 350 waltzes, minuets, landler, ecossaises, other charming, melodic dance compositions reprinted from the authoritative Breitkopf & Härtel edition. 192pp. 9⅜ × 12¼. 26107-7 Pa. **$11.95**

*Available from your music dealer or write for **free** Music Catalog to*
Dover Publications, Inc., Dept. MUBI, 31 East 2nd Street, Mineola, N.Y. 11501.

Dover Piano and Keyboard Editions

ORGAN WORKS, César Franck. Composer's best-known works for organ, including Six Pieces, Trois Pieces, and Trois Chorals. Oblong format for easy use at keyboard. Authoritative Durand edition. 208pp. 11⅜ × 8¼.
25517-4 Pa. **$13.95**

IBERIA AND ESPAÑA: Two Complete Works for Solo Piano, Isaac Albeniz. Spanish composer's greatest piano works in authoritative editions. Includes the popular "Tango." 192pp. 9 × 12. 25367-8 Pa. **$11.95**

GOYESCAS, SPANISH DANCES AND OTHER WORKS FOR SOLO PIANO, Enrique Granados. Great Spanish composer's most admired, most performed suites for the piano, in definitive Spanish editions. 176pp. 9 × 12. 25481-X Pa. **$9.95**

SELECTED PIANO COMPOSITIONS, César Franck, edited by Vincent d'Indy. Outstanding selection of influential French composer's piano works, including early pieces and the two masterpieces–Prelude, Choral and Fugue; and Prelude, Aria and Finale. Ten works in all. 138pp. 9 × 12. 23269-7 Pa. **$10.95**

THE COMPLETE PRELUDES AND ETUDES FOR PIANOFORTE SOLO, Alexander Scriabin. All the preludes and etudes including many perfectly spun miniatures. Edited by K. N. Igumnov and Y. I. Mil'shteyn. 250pp. 9 × 12. 22919-X Pa. **$11.95**

COMPLETE PIANO SONATAS, Alexander Scriabin. All ten of Scriabin's sonatas, reprinted from an authoritative early Russian edition. 256pp. 8¾ × 11¼. 25850-5 Pa. **$12.95**

COMPLETE PRELUDES AND ETUDES-TABLEAUX, Serge Rachmaninoff. Forty-one of his greatest works for solo piano, including the riveting C Minor, G-Minor and B-Minor preludes, in authoritative editions. 208pp. 8¾ × 11¼. 25696-0 Pa. **$11.95**

MOZART MASTERPIECES: 19 WORKS FOR SOLO PIANO, Wolfgang Amadeus Mozart. Superb assortment includes sonatas, fantasies, variations, rondos, minuets, and more. Highlights include "Turkish Rondo," "Sonata in C," and a dozen variations on "Ah, vous dirai-je, Maman" (better known as "Twinkle, Twinkle, Little Star"). Convenient, attractive, inexpensive volume; authoritative sources. 128pp. 9 x 12.
40408-0 Pa. **$8.95**

GYMNOPÉDIES, GNOSSIENNES AND OTHER WORKS FOR PIANO, Erik Satie. The largest Satie collection of piano works yet published, 17 in all, reprinted from the original French editions. 176pp. 9 × 12. (Not available in France or Germany) 25978-1 Pa. **$10.95**

TWENTY SHORT PIECES FOR PIANO (Sports et Divertissements), Erik Satie. French master's brilliant thumbnail sketches–verbal and musical–of various outdoor sports and amusements. English translations, 20 illustrations. Rare, limited 1925 edition. 48pp. 12 × 8⅞. (Not available in France or Germany) 24365-6 Pa. **$6.95**

COMPLETE PRELUDES, IMPROMPTUS AND VALSES-CAPRICES, Gabriel Fauré. Eighteen elegantly wrought piano works in authoritative editions. Only one-volume collection. 144pp. 9 × 12. (Not available in France or Germany) 25789-4 Pa. **$9.95**

PIANO MUSIC OF BÉLA BARTÓK, Series I, Béla Bartók. New, definitive Archive Edition incorporating composer's corrections. Includes *Funeral March* from *Kossuth, Fourteen Bagatelles,* Bartók's break to modernism. 167pp. 9 × 12. (Available in U.S. only) 24108-4 Pa. **$11.95**

PIANO MUSIC OF BÉLA BARTÓK, Series II, Béla Bartók. Second in the Archive Edition incorporating composer's corrections. 85 short pieces *For Children, Two Elegies, Two Romanian Dances,* etc. 192pp. 9 × 12. (Available in U.S. only) 24109-2 Pa. **$11.95**

FRENCH PIANO MUSIC, AN ANTHOLOGY, Isidor Phillipp (ed.). 44 complete works, 1670–1905, by Lully, Couperin, Rameau, Alkan, Saint-Saëns, Delibes, Bizet, Godard, many others; favorites, lesser-known examples, but all top quality. 188pp. 9 × 12. (Not available in France or Germany) 23381-2 Pa. **$12.95**

NINETEENTH-CENTURY EUROPEAN PIANO MUSIC: Unfamiliar Masterworks, John Gillespie (ed.). Difficult-to-find etudes, toccatas, polkas, impromptus, waltzes, etc., by Albéniz, Bizet, Chabrier, Fauré, Smetana, Richard Strauss, Wagner and 16 other composers. 62 pieces. 343pp. 9 × 12. (Not available in France or Germany) 23447-9 Pa. **$19.95**

RARE MASTERPIECES OF RUSSIAN PIANO MUSIC: Eleven Pieces by Glinka, Balakirev, Glazunov and Others, edited by Dmitry Feofanov. Glinka's *Prayer,* Balakirev's *Reverie,* Liapunov's *Transcendental Etude, Op. 11, No. 10,* and eight others–full, authoritative scores from Russian texts. 144pp. 9 × 12. 24659-0 Pa. **$9.95**

HUMORESQUES AND OTHER WORKS FOR SOLO PIANO, Antonín Dvořák. Humoresques, Op. 101, complete, Silhouettes, Op. 8, Poetic Tone Pictures, Theme with Variations, Op. 36, 4 Slavonic Dances, more. 160pp. 9 × 12. 28355-0 Pa. **$10.95**

PIANO MUSIC, Louis M. Gottschalk. 26 pieces (including covers) by early 19th-century American genius. "Bamboula," "The Banjo," other Creole, Negro-based material, through elegant salon music. 301pp. 9¾ × 12. 21683-7 Pa. **$15.95**

SOUSA'S GREAT MARCHES IN PIANO TRANSCRIPTION, John Philip Sousa. Playing edition includes: "The Stars and Stripes Forever," "King Cotton," "Washington Post," much more. 24 illustrations. 111pp. 9 × 12. 23132-1 Pa. **$8.95**

COMPLETE PIANO RAGS, Scott Joplin. All 38 piano rags by the acknowledged master of the form, reprinted from the publisher's original editions complete with sheet music covers. Introduction by David A. Jasen. 208pp. 9 × 12. 25807-6 Pa. **$10.95**

RAGTIME REDISCOVERIES, selected by Trebor Jay Tichenor. 64 unusual rags demonstrate diversity of style, local tradition. Original sheet music. 320pp. 9 × 12. 23776-1 Pa. **$14.95**

RAGTIME RARITIES, edited by Trebor Jay Tichenor. 63 tuneful, rediscovered piano rags by 51 composers (or teams). Does not duplicate selections in *Classic Piano Rags* (Dover, 20469-3). 305pp. 9 × 12. 23157-7 Pa. **$14.95**

CLASSIC PIANO RAGS, selected with an introduction by Rudi Blesh. Best ragtime music (1897–1922) by Scott Joplin, James Scott, Joseph F. Lamb, Tom Turpin, nine others. 364pp. 9 × 12. 20469-3 Pa. **$17.95**

RAGTIME GEMS: Original Sheet Music for 25 Ragtime Classics, edited by David A. Jasen. Includes original sheet music and covers for 25 rags, including three of Scott Joplin's finest: *Searchlight Rag, Rose Leaf Rag* and *Fig Leaf Rag.* 122pp. 9 × 12. 25248-5 Pa. **$9.95**

NOCTURNES AND BARCAROLLES FOR SOLO PIANO, Gabriel Fauré. 12 nocturnes and 12 barcarolles reprinted from authoritative French editions. 208pp. 9¾ × 12¼. (Not available in France or Germany) 27955-3 Pa. **$12.95**

FAVORITE WALTZES, POLKAS AND OTHER DANCES FOR SOLO PIANO, Johann Strauss, Jr. Blue Danube, Tales from Vienna Woods, many other best-known waltzes and other dances. 160pp. 9 × 12. 27851-4 Pa. **$10.95**

SELECTED PIANO WORKS FOR FOUR HANDS, Franz Schubert. 24 separate pieces (16 most popular titles): Three Military Marches, Lebensstürme, Four Polonaises, Four Ländler, etc. Rehearsal numbers added. 273pp. 9 × 12. 23529-7 Pa. **$14.95**

Dover Piano and Keyboard Editions

SHORTER WORKS FOR PIANOFORTE SOLO, Franz Schubert. All piano music except Sonatas, Dances, and a few unfinished pieces. Contains Wanderer, Impromptus, Moments Musicals, Variations, Scherzi, etc. Breitkopf and Härtel edition. 199pp. 9⅜ × 12¼. 22648-4 Pa. **$12.95**

WALTZES AND SCHERZOS, Frédéric Chopin. All of the Scherzos and nearly all (20) of the Waltzes from the authoritative Mikuli edition. Editorial commentary. 160pp. 9 × 12. 24316-8 Pa. **$9.95**

COMPLETE PRELUDES AND ETUDES FOR SOLO PIANO, Frédéric Chopin. All 25 Preludes, all 27 Etudes by greatest composer of piano music. Authoritative Mikuli edition. 192pp. 9 × 12. 24052-5 Pa. **$8.95**

COMPLETE BALLADES, IMPROMPTUS AND SONATAS, Frédéric Chopin. The four Ballades, four Impromptus and three Sonatas. Authoritative Mikuli edition. 192pp. 9 × 12. 24164-5 Pa. **$10.95**

NOCTURNES AND POLONAISES, Frédéric Chopin. 20 *Nocturnes* and 11 *Polonaises* reproduced from the authoritative Mikuli edition for pianists, students, and musicologists. Commentary. 224pp. 9 × 12. 24564-0 Pa. **$10.95**

COMPLETE MAZURKAS, Frédéric Chopin. 51 best-loved compositions, reproduced directly from the authoritative Kistner edition edited by Carl Mikuli. 160pp. 9 × 12. 25548-4 Pa. **$8.95**

FANTASY IN F MINOR, BARCAROLLE, BERCEUSE AND OTHER WORKS FOR SOLO PIANO, Frédéric Chopin. 15 works, including one of the greatest of the Romantic period, the Fantasy in F Minor, Op. 49, reprinted from the authoritative German edition prepared by Chopin's student, Carl Mikuli. 224pp. 8⅜ × 11¼. 25950-1 Pa. **$9.95**

COMPLETE HUNGARIAN RHAPSODIES FOR SOLO PIANO, Franz Liszt. All 19 Rhapsodies reproduced directly from an authoritative Russian edition. All headings, footnotes translated to English. Best one volume edition available. 224pp. 8⅜ × 11¼. 24744-9 Pa. **$11.95**

ANNÉES DE PÈLERINAGE, COMPLETE, Franz Liszt. Authoritative Russian edition of piano masterpieces: *Première Année (Suisse): Deuxième Année (Italie)* and *Venezia e Napoli; Troisième Année,* other related pieces. 288pp. 9⅜ × 12¼. 25627-8 Pa. **$13.95**

COMPLETE ETUDES FOR SOLO PIANO, Series I: Including the Transcendental Etudes, Franz Liszt, edited by Busoni. Also includes Etude in 12 Exercises, 12 Grandes Etudes and Mazeppa. Breitkopf & Härtel edition. 272pp. 8⅜ × 11¼. 25815-7 Pa. **$14.95**

COMPLETE ETUDES FOR SOLO PIANO, Series II: Including the Paganini Etudes and Concert Etudes, Franz Liszt, edited by Busoni. Also includes Morceau de Salon, Ab Irato. Breitkopf & Härtel edition. 192pp. 8⅜ × 11¼. 25816-5 Pa. **$10.95**

SONATA IN B MINOR AND OTHER WORKS FOR PIANO, Franz Liszt. One of Liszt's most performed piano masterpieces, with the six Consolations, ten *Harmonies poetiques et religieuses,* two Ballades and two Legendes. Breitkopf & Härtel edition. 208pp. 8⅜ × 11¼. 26182-4 Pa. **$12.95**

PIANO TRANSCRIPTIONS FROM FRENCH AND ITALIAN OPERAS, Franz Liszt. Virtuoso transformations of themes by Mozart, Verdi, Bellini, other masters, into unforgettable music for piano. Published in association with American Liszt Society. 247pp. 9 × 12. 24273-0 Pa. **$13.95**

MEPHISTO WALTZ AND OTHER WORKS FOR SOLO PIANO, Franz Liszt. Rapsodie Espagnole, Liebestraüme Nos. 1–3, Valse Oubliée No. 1, Nuages Gris, Polonaises Nos. 1 and 2, Grand Galop Chromatique, more. 192pp. 8⅜ × 11¼. 28147-7 Pa. **$13.95**

COMPLETE WORKS FOR PIANOFORTE SOLO, Felix Mendelssohn. Breitkopf and Härtel edition of Capriccio in F# Minor, Sonata in E Major, Fantasy in F# Minor, Three Caprices, Songs without Words, and 20 other works. Total of 416pp. 9⅜ × 12¼. Two-vol. set. 23136-4, 23137-2 Pa. **$23.90**

COMPLETE SONATAS AND VARIATIONS FOR SOLO PIANO, Johannes Brahms. All sonatas, five variations on themes from Schumann, Paganini, Handel, etc. Vienna Gesellschaft der Musikfreunde edition. 178pp. 9 × 12. 22650-6 Pa. **$10.95**

COMPLETE SHORTER WORKS FOR SOLO PIANO, Johannes Brahms. All solo music not in other two volumes. Waltzes, Scherzo in E Flat Minor, Eight Pieces, Rhapsodies, Fantasies, Intermezzi, etc. Vienna Gesellschaft der Musikfreunde. 180pp. 9 × 12. 22651-4 Pa. **$10.95**

COMPLETE TRANSCRIPTIONS, CADENZAS AND EXERCISES FOR SOLO PIANO, Johannes Brahms. Vienna Gesellschaft der Musikfreunde edition, vol. 15. Studies after Chopin, Weber, Bach; gigues, sarabandes; 10 Hungarian dances, etc. 178pp. 9 × 12. 22652-2 Pa. **$12.95**

PIANO MUSIC OF ROBERT SCHUMANN, Series I, edited by Clara Schumann. Major compositions from the period 1830–39; *Papillons, Toccata, Grosse Sonate No. 1, Phantasiestücke, Arabeske, Blumenstück,* and nine other works. Reprinted from Breitkopf & Härtel edition. 274pp. 9⅜ × 12¼. 21459-1 Pa. **$14.95**

PIANO MUSIC OF ROBERT SCHUMANN, Series II, edited by Clara Schumann. Major compositions from period 1838–53; *Humoreske, Novelletten,* Sonate No. 2, 43 *Clavierstücke für die Jugend,* and six other works. Reprinted from Breitkopf & Härtel edition. 272pp. 9⅜ × 12¼. 21461-3 Pa. **$13.95**

PIANO MUSIC OF ROBERT SCHUMANN, Series III, edited by Clara Schumann. All solo music not in other two volumes, including *Symphonic Etudes, Phantaisie,* 13 other choice works. Definitive Breitkopf & Härtel edition. 224pp. 9⅜ × 12¼. 23906-3 Pa. **$11.95**

PIANO MUSIC 1888–1905, Claude Debussy. Deux Arabesques, Suite Bergamesque, Masques, first series of Images, etc. Nine others, in corrected editions. 175pp. 9⅜ × 12¼. 22771-5 Pa. **$8.95**

COMPLETE PRELUDES, Books 1 and 2, Claude Debussy. 24 evocative works that reveal the essence of Debussy's genius for musical imagery, among them many of the composer's most famous piano compositions. Glossary of French terms. 128pp. 8⅜ × 11¼. 25970-6 Pa. **$7.95**

PRELUDES, BOOK I: The Autograph Score, Claude Debussy. Superb facsimile reproduced directly from priceless autograph score in Pierpont Morgan Library in New York. New Introduction by Roy Howat. 48pp. 8¼ × 11. 25549-2 Pa. **$8.95**

PIANO MASTERPIECES OF MAURICE RAVEL, Maurice Ravel. Handsome affordable treasury; *Pavane pour une infante defunte, jeux d'eau, Sonatine, Miroirs,* more. 128pp. 9 × 12. (Not available in France or Germany) 25137-3 Pa. **$8.95**

COMPLETE LYRIC PIECES FOR PIANO, Edvard Grieg. All 66 pieces from Grieg's ten sets of little mood pictures for piano, favorites of generations of pianists. 224pp. 9⅜ × 12¼. 26176-X Pa. **$11.95**